How to Be an Entrepreneur without Even Trying

By Grayson Dearlove

ISBN:1493505505
ISBN-13:9781493505500

DEDICATION

To my family.

In 2013, Grayson Dearlove dissolved a company he started just twenty-two months before—the second failed start-up that he closed in less than two years. Also in 2013, he joined an angel investment group, tried to raise a $150 million venture capital fund, and started three new companies. Meanwhile, another one of his companies—one that he thought was doomed to failure years ago—continued to grow and pay dividends, while yet another of his companies began to wind down after almost ten years of successful operation. Most days he swung from feeling tremendously wealthy and talented to feeling like a failure on the edge of financial ruin. He was forty years old.

It was also in 2013 that he drank literally gallons of coffee during meetings with hundreds of entrepreneurs and investors. He wrote a great business plan for a game-changing technology that nobody understood. He started looking for a corporate job. He puzzled over the ridiculous start-ups that were being funded daily on the West Coast. He cursed at the almost weekly announcements of new start-up incubators. He sat through dozens of panel discussions on entrepreneurship with "experts" giving the same bad advice. He consulted. He pondered what it meant to be an entrepreneur. He wondered why he was here.

It was against this backdrop of confusion and beauty that he began asking tough questions like:

"Are there no good entrepreneurs, just lucky entrepreneurs?"

"Is it a good thing that so many people are trying to be entrepreneurs?"

"Why is *Who Moved My Cheese* still on the *New York Times* business best seller list?"

Standing at the crossroads of entrepreneurs, angel investors, and venture capitalists, Dr. Dearlove realized he had useful insights about start-ups that few others could offer. He had been living in all three worlds at the same time. He began to laugh about himself and the whole start-up ecosystem. And he wrote this book. There was no stopping the tide of new entrepreneurs, so why not try to help them?

How to Be an Entrepreneur without Even Trying is a resource for entrepreneurs, wantrepreneurs, and investors alike. It teaches lessons by exposing absurdity. The ambitious reader can use this guide to launch a successful big-impact, high-growth business in any sector, regardless of educational background, level of experience, or ability.

CONTENTS

Introduction x

1 - Wantrepreneurs 1

2 - Which Idea to Pursue 4

3 – Avoiding Early Mistakes 8

4 - Do Not Quit your Job . . . Yet 12

5 - Market Research 15

6 - Naming your Baby 19

7 - Choosing a Partner 21

8 - Writing the Business Plan 27

9 - Negotiating with your Partner 36

10 - Start-Up Lawyers 38

11 - The Pitch Book 40

12 - The Elevator Pitch 42

13 - Find your Angels 44

14 - The Dog and Pony Show 48

15 - Sealing the Deal 55

16 - First Hires Make Great Pets 57

17 - Why You Need Customers 59

18 - Seducing the VC 61

19 - Negotiating a Term Sheet..66

20 - The Power of Press Releases..70

21 - Breaking up with your Cofounder..73

22 - The Series B Club..77

23 - Series C Shopping Spree..80

24 - The Exit..82

25 - Screw-you Money..84

26 - Bang! You are a Brand and a Mentor...................................87

27 - Glossary for Entrepreneurs...90

How to Be an Entrepreneur without Even Trying

By Grayson Dearlove

Illustrated by Rick Menard

INTRODUCTION

In this age of fast-paced change, the enterprising entrepreneur needs a quick reference guide to help navigate the start-up landscape and conquer the business world. This book provides enlightening insights, bold advice, and easy-to-implement strategies for the twenty-first-century entrepreneur. While some may naively label this work as frivolous because of its witty pace, you should not be fooled! Underlying each chapter are key lessons that were developed through years of trial and error and by keen observations by the author, an entrepreneur and investor blessed with many successes and many failures.

This book will serve as your trusted companion on your way to entrepreneurial success and renown. You do not need an MBA—or even a college degree for that matter. If you are of average intelligence and have a good work ethic and outsized ambitions, this guide is all you need to succeed as an entrepreneur. If you have above-average intelligence and advanced degrees, all the better. This will make your climb to the top easier and quicker.

The lessons presented here have been time-tested by contemporary entrepreneurs of every make, model, and creed and by people of all ages. It is never too late, nor is it ever too early, to launch your venture and secure the screw-you money (see Chapter 25) you richly deserve. This guide covers most contingencies you may encounter and can be applied to businesses as varied as cloud security and virtual diapers. This book can be used to equal effect by men or women. If you have experience in sales, you may find the nuanced strategies easier to master because this is what entrepreneurs do: They sell. All day, every day. They sell to partners, employees, investors, customers, spouses, and themselves. The spirited entrepreneur wakes up selling and falls asleep to dream of selling more!

For the investor, this guide offers insights into the next wave of entrepreneurs who will be pitching to you. To understand their clever strategies and motivations, read this guide carefully. It will also allow you to shake the antiquated criteria and herd mentality that has been costing you real dollars for many years. To be a better investor, you must thoroughly understand this animal that is the entrepreneur. This book dissects and exposes the best strategies of this complex beast.

1 - WANTREPRENEURS

A wantrepreneur is someone who is always talking about great business ideas, but he or she has yet to follow through and start a business or join a start-up. Instead, he gets himself all wound up about perceived wonderfully novel products and services, only to lose interest and move on to a new idea after a few weeks.

"I had a great idea last night. Listen, this thing is going to make us a ton of money."

"Really? What idea this time?"

"You promise not to tell anybody?"

"Of course."

"It's a mirror application for smart phones."

"A mirror app?"

"Yeah, it's a mirror app for checking your hair and makeup when you don't have a mirror on you."

"Why not just use the forward-facing camera that is common on most phones now?"

"You could do that, but this is a mirror. It turns your screen into a mirror."

"I don't know if that's a good idea or not. And aren't there already apps like this?"

"You just don't get it yet. I must not be explaining it well."

Wantrepreneurs love to crash events for entrepreneurs and start-ups, but they are not necessarily bad people. It is OK to be a wantrepreneur. In fact, a study by the Kuaffman Institute showed that 94.5 percent of all entrepreneurs were wantrepreneurs before they became actual entrepreneurs. And the wantrepreneur has much more in common with the real entrepreneur than most corporate animals.

Surround yourself with wantrepreneurs because they are usually great company—creative and passionate and even more so after a few drinks. Some of your best friends may be wantrepreneurs, you may have dated wantrepreneurs, and you are probably in denial about being a wantrepreneur.

To the keen observer, some telltale signs of the wantrepreneur include: enjoys recapping episodes of *Shark Tank* for his friends and colleagues; privately refers to his current employer's upper-management team using terms like "idiots," "clueless," and "stupid"; in describing somebody else's successful start-up, can be heard saying, "I just don't get it; I came up with that idea years ago"; frequently ends the description of his ideas with the phrase "we would make so much money."

The good news is that this book can turn wantrepreneurs into successful entrepreneurs. If that is your intent, read on.

2 - WHICH IDEA TO PURSUE

There is nothing more important to your journey from wantrepreneur zero to entrepreneur hero than choosing the right idea. A common misperception is that great ideas strike quickly and randomly. This is rarely the case. Most great ideas organically develop over time from the diligent pursuit of bad ideas.

The idea must be big enough to eventually get you a guest spot on CNBC, but not so big and complicated that it is impossible to execute. Equally important: The idea must have a huge market—either one currently existing or one that evolves from your brilliant, inspired insights.

There are three reasons for these conditions: 1) It takes as much time and effort to build a $10 million revenue business as it does to build a $1 billion revenue business, so go big or go home; 2) you want to pursue this with other people's money, and they will only invest if your idea has big money-making potential; 3) you want a by-product of your eventual success to be an ample amount of screw-you money—the kind of money that you have dreamt about since your first crappy boss. Screw-you money only comes in one flavor: scalable ideas that address huge markets. Of course, money should not be your primary motivation, but never deny yourself this important perk!

Also helpful, but not entirely required, is that your idea should address a need or a problem in a market you know something about. This is not necessary if you are of average intelligence and a quick learner. The resourceful entrepreneur can hire all the industry expertise she needs.

The eventual product must also be "sticky." That is, whoever buys it will want to keep buying it from you because the costs of switching are just too painful. Insurance businesses and cable TV providers long ago mastered the sticky product; it takes so much effort to change providers that customers infrequently do so. You may have heard something about the importance of customer retention and recurring revenue. The solution is a sticky product. Ideally--from a business perspective--sticky products lead to a monopoly.

Do not look for your idea at the local university. Better entrepreneurs than you have been enamored by the romantic vision of helping the absent-minded professor commercialize Flubber. Alas, such stories are best left to the silver screen. University-owned technologies are quicksand for start-ups. They are best for licensing by established companies, not for spinning out new companies.

The problem lies in the professor as founder. Do not be drawn in by his impressive subject-matter knowledge and authoritative tone! Of all the creatures that grace the earth, the academic is the least suited to starting and growing successful businesses. Combine no business experience with a large ego, add a dash of chasing tenure and a sprinkle of way too busy, and you have a great recipe for wasting your time. The start-up is more of a hobby to them. Having been successful at all things academic their whole lives, they think business is easy and "based on common sense." They believe that if they can figure out how to get published two dozen times, they can surely figure out how to build a business. Nothing could be further from the truth.

The other reality is this: Any academic that might be worth partnering with will have figured out how to develop technology and start companies outside the reach of their university. These clever chaps may be worth partnering with but will not be found through the university technology transfer office.

HELP YOURSELF!
AS THE PROFESSOR SAYS... GO AHEAD!
PATENTS
TECH TRANSFER

3 – AVOIDING EARLY MISTAKES

Your mother may have told you that you should not keep secrets, and if she was giving start-up advice, she was right. At the formative stages of your business it is imperative that you solicit and receive feedback on your idea from peers that you respect. This early in the game, believe it or not, there are others who know more about your business idea than you do. Listen to them! Nothing will waste more of your time than a "good" idea that you can't explain.

The trick here is to flesh out the idea quickly and thoroughly before wasting precious resources on a plan doomed to failure. That's right. Your time is precious! You may not know it, but you only have so many chances at this, so you absolutely cannot afford to waste your time chasing a bad idea. Spend the time up front and you will be happy you did.

Binge Networking

Binge networking is like when you first put your profile up on match.com: You don't do it for the casual sex, but you don't mind it. Network your tail off to find potential partners, investors, dates, and so on. Networking is never a waste of time—especially when there's an open bar.

"Hi! My name's Ollie."

"Hi Ollie. I'm Teresa."

"Teresa, please tell me something interesting or I may just melt."

[Laughter] "Ha! I know the feeling! I'm been hovering around the food to try to blend in."

"Seriously, tell me something interesting."

"OK. I'm pretty sure that guy over there is pretending to talk on his cell phone to avoid conversations."

[Ollie bursts into laughter.]

"Thanks for the laugh, Teresa. That is funnier than a grown man playing jazz flute. What do you do for a living?"

After a couple dozen of these awkward conversations, you will become quite proficient at networking and may even come to enjoy the sport.

Learning a New Market

If your idea applies to an industry you know very little about, do not be deterred. Simply spend a few hours performing market research using the Google machine. You will be amazed at what you can learn on the Internet—and some of it is true! Regardless, you can quickly pick up the buzzwords needed to be fluent in any industry after only a few days.

"Of course, this represents a new enhanced consumer engagement platform that will optimize production tools across your SaaS businesses."

"It's obviously a brilliant automated real-time behavior tracking application that offers predictive social intelligence solutions that will dramatically impact bottom lines."

"We have developed an innovative customer engagement alerting and incident management tool to help midsized businesses improve their marketing ROI."

And so on. Use similar phrases authoritatively when talking with people about your idea. Remember the point is to get feedback at this stage, even if you don't completely understand the idea or the market. If that is the case, don't worry—the experts you ask will explain it to you!

Poison Ivy in a Can

Do not confuse inventions with businesses. You may invent a way to do something that is completely new and innovative. It may even be patentable. But does it create value that people will want in exchange for money?

Here's an example: You have just figured out how to isolate and aerosolize urushiol, the active chemical in poison ivy. What an innovation! You apply for and receive a patent for poison ivy in a can. There must be a killer app for this novel invention, if only you can find the right market. Alas, universities make this mistake all of the time.

Honestly Assess Early Feedback

If you repeatedly receive lukewarm feedback to your idea, or if it takes you more than two minutes to explain, you should reconsider the whole venture. You need to hear enthusiastic responses with exclamation points! Some desirable responses include:

"Wow, Ollie! That is the best idea I've heard in a long time!"

"Ollie, I really think you're on to something!"

"That makes me want to dance!"

Anything less and you should go back to the drawing board. But do not be discouraged. You are full of good ideas. Simply reset and try again. Remember, great ideas are born from the relentless pursuit of bad ideas.

The Non-Disclosure Agreement (NDA)

While still in the idea stage, the enterprising entrepreneur should steer clear of the nondisclosure agreement (NDA), also known as a confidential disclosure agreement (CDA). Pursuing the execution of this document will make you look bad and cost you friends! Requesting such agreements reeks of amateur hour. Rest assured, if your idea is so fragile that it can be stolen and replicated by another so easily, the idea was never going to work anyway. So seek out your trusted friends and advisers and speak freely to get some real feedback. Save the NDA for later.

4 - DO NOT QUIT YOUR JOB . . . YET

Now that you have your idea, you may think it's time to jump in with both feet and quit your day job. Do not make this mistake! At this stage it is much too early to cut the cord with your stodgy employer. A better strategy is to hold on to your day job until the very last minute, lest you find yourself with no income, growing expenses, and no outside investment—a probable path to failure!

Going all in at this point is too risky and inadvisable. Keep your activities to yourself for a few months while you flesh out your idea. Then, when it looks like your idea has legs and you need to spend more time on it, you can casually mention it to your boss over cake in the break room. Be sure not to get into specifics when discussing your outside activities with your boss. It is the best way to avoid uncomfortable questions.

"Yes, Mr. Stackhouse. I've been looking into a couple of ideas during my off hours. Nothing too intense—I'm just trying to learn as much as I can about business in general."

"That's fine, Ollie! I had no idea you were so interested in business."

"Yes, quite interested, sir. I've always wondered what it would be like to run a business. Of course it would be easy for someone as knowledgeable as you, but I'm still learning. It is a ways off for me, of course, but it is an interest of mine."

"Wonderful! Your ambition is refreshing, Ollie. Just let me know how I can help."

Now you have bought yourself time and gained an important ally. Such a blessing from your boss should be taken as permission to access all of your current company's resources to pursue your idea. Broadband, phone, office supplies, conference rooms, and so on—feel free to use these resources as needed. Your boss would be proud of your initiative! As an added benefit, you will get credit for working long hours, even if the extra time at the office is due to your new start-up.

"Working late, Ollie?"

"Yes, Mr. Stackhouse. I was finishing up my analysis on the Corbomite Project."

"Good job, Ollie. Don't stay too late."

It is always best to do outside work during normal business hours and perform your actual duties after hours or on weekends. Mr. Stackhouse does not need to know that you spent most of your regular business hours performing market research for your new idea. He does not care about such details, just as long as the work gets done. And he will be greatly impressed that you are working so hard on the weekends for his company!

If any of your colleagues start to catch on and ask questions, just act annoyed and say you are too busy to talk. Always act busy—perception is reality!

It is important to defer start-up expenses for as long as possible. Never feel guilty about borrowing resources, as your current employer will enjoy sharing their infrastructure with such a fine employee! You may consider it part of your compensation for years of dedicated loyalty. Also, your employer will bask in the good press they will get once you are successful and your bio mentions you worked there.

5 - MARKET RESEARCH

So what can you do to advance your start-up while you are still gainfully employed? Market research, of course. In addition to verbal feedback on your idea, which you garner during breaks and luncheons away from your day job, you will need to collect evidence about the potential market for your products. You also need to identify and evaluate competitors in the space and other start-ups that may be nibbling at the edges of your grand idea. Such research involves intense Google searches for free market reports, news articles, and blogs. You may even need to go to your local university and borrow its subscriptions to premier news and market research databases. The purpose is twofold: 1) to convince yourself that there is a real opportunity for your idea to succeed, and 2) to start collecting the evidence that will convince investors.

Caution: At this stage you still need to maintain your BS filter. You are still trying to determine if this is the idea you want to wrap your ego and reputation around for the next several years. Do not bullshit yourself! There is plenty of time for that later. Listen to feedback and ask a lot of questions. You have to believe that the market will be there AND you are the person to execute. Remember, you will eventually have to sell something to be successful.

During this deep dive, one of two things will happen: You will become convinced that you have a tiger by the tail, or you will become more confused than ever about the quality of your idea. If the latter happens, it is time to abandon it and start working on another. But do not be discouraged. It is much better to abandon a bad idea sooner rather than later. Do not think you have wasted your time. Quite the contrary—you will have learned valuable lessons that can be applied to the next idea. Simply go back to Chapter 2 to brush up on idea development, and try again.

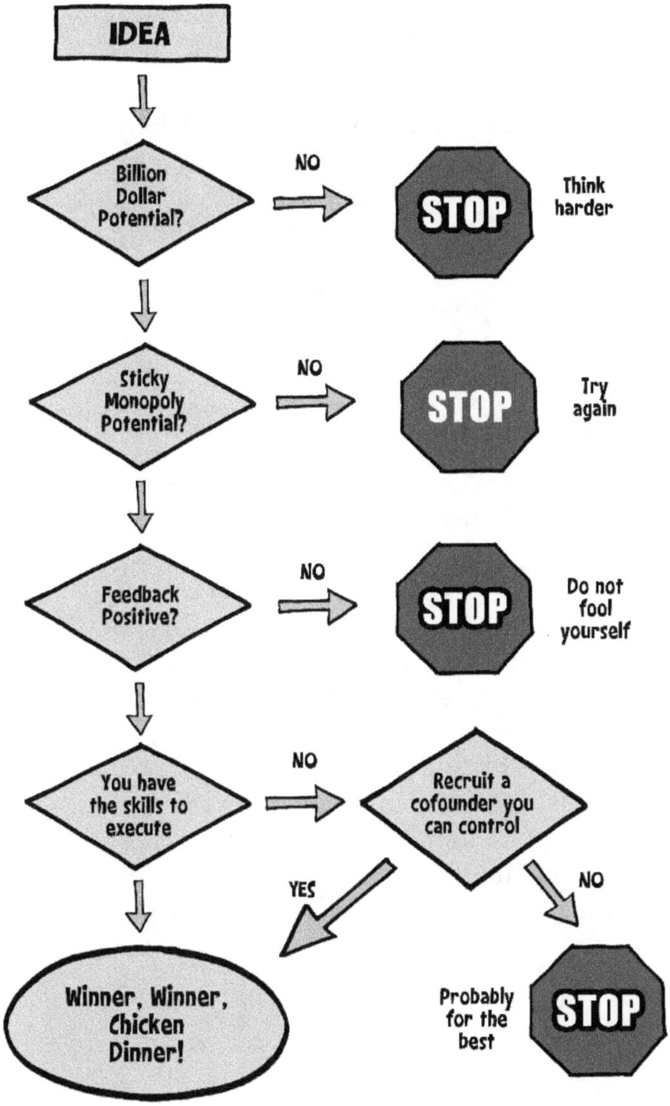
IDEA
Billion Dollar Potential?
NO
STOP
Think harder
Sticky Monopoly Potential?
NO
STOP
Try again
Feedback Positive?
NO
STOP
Do not fool yourself
You have the skills to execute
NO
Recruit a cofounder you can control
YES
NO
Winner, Winner, Chicken Dinner!
Probably for the best
STOP

One final pitfall to be aware of while garnering feedback: People are much more likely to react positively than negatively because there is little upside for them in hurting your feelings. So evaluate the feedback you receive through a prism of skepticism.

"Gosh, Ollie! I think that is a grand vision."

"T-Bone, I need your honest feedback on this. You will not hurt my feelings if you don't like it."

"No, really, Ollie. I think it's great. You should go for it."

"You're sure? What specifically do you like about it?"

"I like the way you tell the story about the customer pain point. It's funny. You're a funny guy. That idea is 100 percent great."

Such overly positive feedback without proper inquiry or explanation should be ignored. You want probing questions from smart skeptics during discussions. You want to impress your evaluator with your well-thought-out answers. Turning a skeptic from a "no" to a "yes" is the most positive data point you can gather.

If after substantial research into your idea you are still very bullish, then congratulations! It is time to proceed.

6 - NAMING YOUR BABY

[Note: Trademark lawyers will tell you that the best and most recognizable trademarks are exactly one or two words long. Their advice on this topic is valid and should be followed, so go with a name that is short and simple.]

Decide on a company name before settling on a partner or writing the business plan. Doing so has several advantages: 1) It gives the company a separate identity from you and immediately makes it sound like a big operation; 2) it firmly establishes you as the lead dog of this enterprise; you do not need to listen to "but I came up with the name" arguments when negotiating with partners; and 3) the tone of the business plan will sound more authoritative if a proper name has been established.

The name really does matter, mostly because you never want to go through the hell of changing it. Spend some time and come up with a good one. Remember that this name will someday become a part of everyday lexicon, so do not underestimate the challenge. It must be simple and catchy, and the best ones have absolutely nothing to do with what the business actually does. Do not make up a name that no one can pronounce or a name that can be pronounced several different ways. You will quickly tire of correcting people and spelling it on the phone. Instead, pick a name that is both readable and unique by combining two common words that have no reason to be together like “Floating Rocks, Inc.,” “Straight Curves, Inc.,” “Dead Cat, Inc.,” “Microsoft,” or “Led Zeppelin.” You get the idea.

Before settling on a name you must do three other things: 1) confirm the domain name is available, 2) search the patent and trademark office website to uncover any existing trademarks, and 3) say it out loud twelve times in a row without it sounding stupid. If the name clears these hurdles, register the domain name and start thinking about a clever logo.

7 - CHOOSING A PARTNER

Finding a good business partner greatly increases the odds that your new venture will succeed. You want a partner to help you make better decisions and share the early workload during the company's formative years. Eventually, your executive team and BOD will fill this role. But early on, a good partner will prove invaluable. Choosing a partner is second in importance only to choosing your idea. Just look for one partner. It is easier to part ways with one partner later rather than multiple partners, as will be necessary.

Primary Qualities to Look for in Your Partner

The most important qualities to look for in your partner are reasonableness and good temperament. You will be spending a lot of time with your partner (perhaps several years), so you must enjoy his or her company. As you grow your business, your relationship will be constantly tested. And you will argue—probably a lot. You want a partner with whom you can have a heated discussion one minute and then share a laugh over a beer soon after. A person who holds grudges will not do at all. Nor will people who are prone to unreasonable and illogical behavior. You need a partner with consistency of character. You need someone who you are comfortable firing. This means you can count on her. You should know how she will react to situations before she does. This is a key ingredient in managing your new partner.

Secondary Qualities to Look for in Your Partner

Of secondary importance are qualities such as previous start-up experience, intelligence, industry contacts, skills you do not have, and so on. If you cannot get along well with your partner, all of these qualities are of little value. Of course it is nice to find a partner with skill sets complimentary to your own, but this is gravy.

Caution: A partner with better industry contacts than you threatens to be of more importance to the venture than you. Avoid this situation at all costs! Likewise, a partner who is more clever than you may outmaneuver you during critical periods of company growth—another situation to be avoided! So find a partner who will be *almost* as valuable to the venture as you.

Where to Find Your Partner

Your partner should be an acquaintance just outside your circle of friends. It is risky indeed to try to start a business with a close friend. Successful start-ups blow up preexisting friendships. They just do, so do not attempt this journey with a good friend. Besides, there are plenty of quality candidates in your network, so there is no need to risk losing a good friend during your climb to the top.

THE
Partner Store
OPEN 24/7
START-UPS
GET
HALF
OFF!

Start with your LinkedIn network. Who in your network do you respect, trust, have lunch with occasionally, latch on to at uncomfortable networking events, and so on? Target these people as potential partners. Avoid anyone with a LinkedIn profile picture that appears to have been taken by a camera they were holding.

"Karen, I had an idea I wanted to run by you. How about lunch next week?"

"Sure, Ollie. I look forward to catching up."

"Stu, I was hoping to get your feedback on something. You want to grab a drink after work?"

"Of course, I'd be glad to help."

And then you spring it on them. This is your first sales pitch—and a critical one!

Timing

Only approach your potential partner once you have received adequate feedback about your idea and you are 95 percent sure you will be pursuing it. You do not want to use up opportunities to dazzle a potential partner with ideas that you never end up pursuing. This may cause them to lose faith in you and could dampen your chances of landing them in the future. It is also good to engage a potential partner before writing the business plan. While you will do most of the writing, you do want your partner to feel like they have some input to instill some pride of ownership.

What to Do If You Are Approached to Be a Partner

Being an industrious and talented person, you may be approached by another before you find the right idea for your own company. Beware of the colleague who asks for feedback over coffee, for this is usually the start of their partnership soft sell. Listen politely and give them your opinion, suggestions, and encouragement. But show little enthusiasm for the idea, even if you love it. Also talk about how terribly busy you are pursuing your own venture (keep it vague). This will put you in a better position to negotiate with your suitor if it goes that far.

"Ollie, thanks for meeting me for coffee. I want to tell you about a start-up I'm working on to see if you might want to get involved."

"Sounds mighty interesting, Denise, but unfortunately I have no bandwidth right now. Between work at Stackhouse Industries and my new venture, I am spread thin."

"I understand, but please hear me out."

"Of course, I am happy to help around the edges if I can. It's just a bandwidth thing, I assure you."

If the idea presented to you is big, bold, and excites you—and you can add value—go ahead and entertain the partnership offer. Becoming the minority partner of a promising venture has these benefits: 1) It addresses the fact that you have yet to develop any original high-impact business ideas yourself; 2) you gain valuable experience being second banana that will eventually help you on your way to becoming top banana; 3) the minority partner often walks away with the best deal; they reap the financial rewards of success without all of the stress and responsibility of the CEO.

Keep in mind that you will eventually have a painful falling out with this person asking you to be a partner—probably in year three or four—so be sure to pre-negotiate accelerated vesting and other beneficial severance terms. Getting forced out will sting, but it is actually a desirable outcome. You can maintain your upside in the business without dealing with the day-to-day BS. And then you can move on to your next venture—your venture—a wiser person.

If the idea presented is a dog, let them down easy. But like Patrick Swayze says in *Roadhouse,* always "be nice." Never tell a person directly you think their idea is terrible. No need to hurt his or her feelings, and, besides, you may need this person later. Take a lesson from the venture capitalist world here. It has perfected saying "no" without saying "no." Instead, tell your suitor that "it seems like a very interesting opportunity" and that you will have to think about it and get back to them (you won't). Think about it until they move on to asking another person.

8 - WRITING THE BUSINESS PLAN

The proper sequence for developing investor materials is: Prepare the business plan first, the pitch book second, and the elevator pitch last. When you proceed from the most detailed document to the simplest, you communicate more effectively.

There are hundreds of business plan competitions across the United States to enter annually. Do not waste your time with them. While a $20,000 first prize of in-kind services may seem appealing, chasing such fool's gold is a huge distraction. Instead of spending hours iterating your business plan for judges who are usually lawyers and accountants, you should focus on getting traction with customers and quickly finishing a tight business plan for your investors' interns to read. Luckily, everything you need to know about effective business plan writing is presented in this short chapter.

The business plan has value for two reasons: 1) It forces you to carefully consider all aspects of the business and your vision for what it can become; and 2) it is a basic requirement for raising outside capital. No need to fight the system here, as you will benefit from writing it. And be sure you take the lead over your business partner in the writing of the business plan. This is important posturing, as you will see in the next chapter.

Follow the rules outlined here to write the best business plan in the least amount of time. Never forget: Your time is your most precious resource, even at this early stage. Spend it wisely!

What follows are the only five things you need to know about business plans:

1. No one of any importance will read past the executive summary.
2. The purpose of the executive summary is to get you a meeting.
3. The whole thing is a sales document. The product is your start-up and you are selling it to investors and your partner (the only people who may read past the executive summary).
4. The full business plan should be no longer than twenty pages.
5. The business plan should only contain these five sections: Secret Sauce, Market, Business Model, Team, and Financials.

Secret Sauce

The Secret Sauce section describes the pain point your business idea addresses and then describes how your innovative solution (secret sauce) solves this problem for customers. Here you will present a summary of your product, how wonderful it works, and any traction that you have gotten thus far. It will also include some technical details about your secret sauce and your intellectual property (IP) position. For any business other than software or internet-related, investors will require you to have an IP position; a hollow provisional patent should satisfy at this point.

"Dead Cat, Inc., has a revolutionary approach to CRM that solves a major pain point of every large business using a customer-centric approach that results in a 50 percent cost reduction and a 70 percent increase in sales."

Do not give away too much information here, as you never know where this document may end up! The interns who read your plan may work for firms that have other portfolio companies operating in similar markets. The ambitious intern may try to make associate by stealing some clever feature of your product and suggesting to a partner that it be introduced through one of their existing portfolio companies. Since there is no NDA in place yet, you will have no recourse. Thus, it is best to leave much unsaid. To conclude the Secret Sauce section, say something like: "More information available upon request." (They never request more information—you either get a meeting, or you don't.)

Market

The Market section is where you describe the largess of the market opportunity. For starters, the eventual market size must be larger than $1 billion annually. Anything less is not worth investor's time. When describing the market, quotes from experts with important-sounding titles are useful, as are projections from market reports showing double-digit growth over the next ten years. Nobody ever follows up on the accuracy of market research companies, so do not worry if the numbers look fishy. Because you have a reference, your numbers will not be questioned.

The best market data you can present is indirect market data. This is "data" that has been collected from a number of different sources that you bundle to "prove" the existence of the market. This data is so valuable because it allows you to inconspicuously derive conclusions based on assumptions you create. And assumptions are like strong opinions—they are hard to argue against. When you present indirect market data, use flashy graphics to hide the underlying weakness of the actual data. Remember, you can make an attractive trend line from just two data points. As long as you have references, investors will be impressed by your ingenuity in calculating the market size.

You should also discuss the competitive landscape in the Market section. Listing five or six competitors will be satisfactory. Focus on competitors that people might know and focus on why they are doing a lousy job of addressing this market opportunity. Use a chart with green, yellow, and red "stoplights" showing competitors across the top and product features down the side—this is always a crowd-pleaser. Be sure your own company column is full of green lights while competitors' columns are littered with red ones.

"Dead Cat, Inc., operates here in this fourth quadrant of the market, which is clearly huge but unaddressable by BigCo's because of their lack of innovation."

Never try to indicate that you "have no direct competitors." This trick has been tried by better men and women than you, and investors hate this answer even if it is true. It comes across as either hubris or laziness, and it makes them uncomfortable. It is far better to feed them some competitive decoys, even if there are no competitors (or market) for your product yet.

Business Model

In the Business Model section you describe how your company will make money. Simpler is better. Investors do not want you adding risk by proposing some exotic business model that has never been tried before. Despite the hype around innovative business models like Google and Groupon, these are outliers. It is much safer and preferable to keep the business model basic. Complex business models are difficult to communicate and will most likely be lost on your investors anyway.

Flowcharts that describe your business model are desirable here. Use lots of arrows and dollar signs showing inflows of money to your company. Also in this section, be sure to discuss your business's very large margins and easy scalability. Anything less than 50 percent margins will not impress.

It is also appropriate to discuss your go-to-market strategy. Your extensive knowledge of the customer, and the emerging market, should dazzle your reader and jump off the page. Be sure to include a reasonable estimate of customer acquisition costs. This will really get you bonus points!

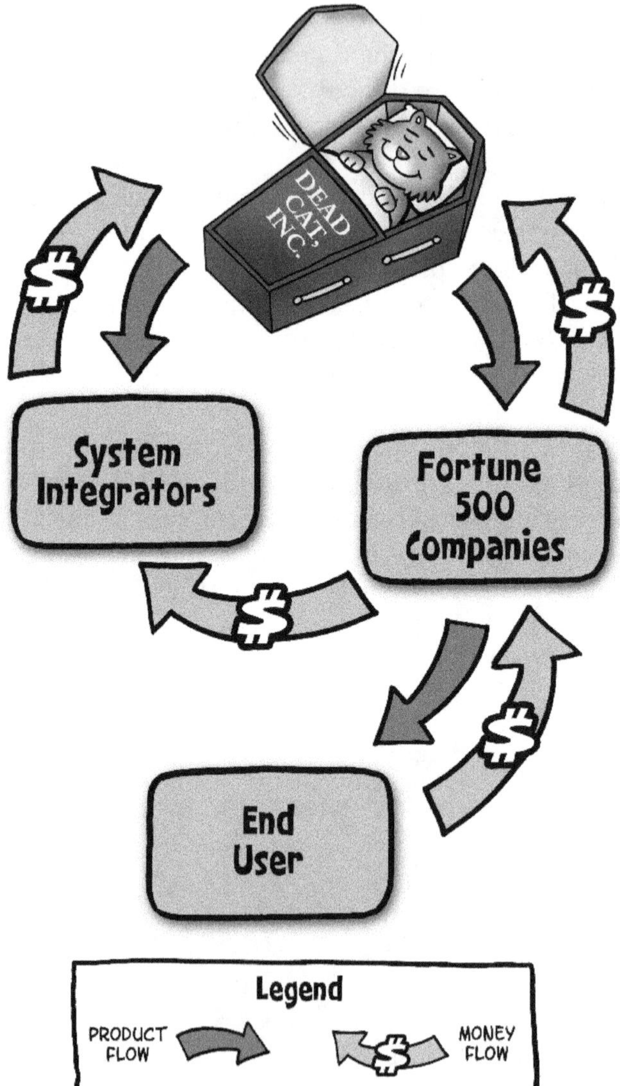
DEAD CAT, INC.
System Integrators
Fortune 500 Companies
End User
Legend
PRODUCT FLOW
MONEY FLOW

Team

It is time to beat your chest a little and talk about how great the team is. While misrepresentations are not allowed, exaggerations are recommended. In the full business plan, every team member should have at least a three-paragraph biography—any shorter and investors may question their credentials.

Aggressively hyping your team here has an added benefit: It makes it less likely that investors will try to mess with it. Preemptively convince investors how great your team is to avoid having them try to "add value" by tinkering with the team you have handpicked.

Make sure that any time you are talking about the team, you pepper the conversation with phrases like "really good chemistry," "complementary skill sets," and "work really well together." This sets up the investor for when he or she eventually gets around to looking at the bios. After you leave a room, you want people to say, "Rock-star team! If anyone can pull this off, they can." "Rock-star" is preferable to "world-class," although both will work.

Because of your good work on the Team section, you have teed up your canned answer to the question you will get at every other meeting.

"Ollie, what's to prevent BigCo from doing the same thing a slightly different way?"

"Great question, sir."
[Long pause.]

"It's the team. Nobody has this rock-star team. This team knows this market better than anyone on the planet, and we all work well together because of our complementary skill sets. The Lord loves a working man, and this team works."

No need to mention that your CTO is a drunk and the CFO is going through a divorce and dating the twenty-two-year-old programmer. Stick to the business facts! This team you surround yourself with is top-notch!

Financials

The Financials section has exposed many entrepreneurs as wantrepreneurs and stopped them dead in their tracks. Do not let this happen to you! Writing the Financials section takes discipline and separates the grown-ups from the children. If you are spreadsheet challenged, just try to have some fun with it. In fact, this is the section in which you can be the most creative. Drawing numbers from thin air based on assumptions you invent—what could be more fun? You have the freedom of a toddler in art class.

Just as you would describe a believable imaginary friend, you should present your financials in great detail. They should be thorough, and the pro forma should cover at least five years of operations. Use a basic spreadsheet template developed by someone smarter than you to spare yourself the trouble of extracting a clean balance sheet, statement of cash flows, and income statement from the mess. While your model is mostly a fiction, it is a necessity and provides the investor with the inputs for his own models.

To build a pro forma, you must first think through and list major milestones in order to tie them to funding and company finances. Fear not! Lean on your partner for this. Plot your company's personnel needs so that salaries are tied to hiring requirements to sustain growth. This is another great task to assign to your partner so that he or she feels included. Finally, you must make pricing and sales volume assumptions. Do not state the number of customers your financials assume; it will set up a popular question from wily investors.

As long as you can explain your numbers, you will find a receptive audience. Nobody knows more about your business plan than you, so most will defer to your expert judgment when assessing your assumptions. But be careful not to go too far. You want to show impressive—but not unrealistic—financials. Showing revenue projections greater than $50 million in year four will draw unwanted attention. It is just gosh-darn difficult to grow that fast, and investors know it. The savvy entrepreneur leaves outrageous revenue numbers for later pro formas. Always mention that your financials represent a conservative estimate. This is expected and adds to your credibility.

"Ollie, can you comment on the reasonableness of these revenue projections?"

Even though the numbers in the pro forma are comparable to the nutritional value of cigarettes, you are confident.

"Yes, sir. Fine question. The team feels very comfortable that these numbers are very conservative and represent the slowest possible growth scenario."

Your financials should conclude with the proposed "use of funds" from the investment. You can never be too specific here, but bury any salary or benefits for yourself under the heading SG&A. Do not show a burn rate; instead, this is another good question to leave as bait for the live meeting.

9 - NEGOTIATING WITH YOUR PARTNER

Now that the plan is written, you have positioned yourself perfectly for negotiating the company ownership structure with your partner. It is your original business idea and you are the primary author of the business plan. You have done enough work to establish yourself as the dominant partner, yet the business is still more abstract than real. This is good, because it's much easier to negotiate over imaginary money than real money. Rather than argue too hard, your partner will prefer to let you have the majority ownership of something currently worth nothing, if that is what you suggest.

"Well, Pincus, I think it is clear based on how the business plan writing went that I'm doing most of the work, so it's fair that I own most of the company, for now."

Be sure to add "for now," because it gives the illusion that ownership structure between you two could change in the future. But it won't.

"That makes sense, Ollie."

"And of course the whole thing was my idea. But I want

to give you substantial ownership because I really feel like you will eventually be contributing a lot."

Always make it seem like you are being very generous, and phrase it in such a way as to convey that ownership is yours to "give."

"Sure. I appreciate it, Ollie."

"Pincus, a 70-30 split seems a fair starting point. Don't you agree?"

Again, by adding "starting point" you give your partner comfort that she or he could own more of the company if things really take off and the partner starts contributing more. Of course your partner will never own more than is proposed here. But the hope of it is effective for motivational purposes.

10 - START-UP LAWYERS

Business lawyers are eager to sign promising young start-ups as clients, and they will enjoy buying you lunch to discuss your new venture. You should pick a firm with a good reputation for working with start-ups locally, with a preference toward midsized shops. Midsized firms are best because they are small enough that everyone there must still be good at their jobs, but they are big enough to have a strong network. And having a good network is how a good start-up lawyer earns his or her money. You do not need a business lawyer to read NDAs or other simple contracts. You need him or her to make introductions to investors and customers. Eventually, if things go well, you will need this lawyer to review investment documents like term sheets, PPMs, and stockholder agreements.

You should get free lunches from at least three different firms before making a decision, and then go with the firm that takes you to the nicest restaurant. Remember at these luncheons to get all the advice you can, because as soon as you sign an Engagement Agreement, the free lunches are over and these conversations will cost you real dollars! The smart entrepreneur defers as many of these billable hours as possible.

For the high-growth business you are about to build, you will set up a Delaware C corporation. C Corps are the preferred structure for accommodating outside investors, and Delaware is beloved for its extensive business case law (and no sales tax). Have your new law firm file the Articles of Incorporation, issue company shares, and administer the Shareholders Agreement. It will probably cost you around $1,500, but it is well worth it to pay a professional for this tedious work.

If this is your first venture, congratulate yourself after the papers are signed. You have completed your metamorphosis from wantrepreneur to entrepreneur. At this moment, you are beautiful! Enjoy being beautiful for a little while, but then get back to it because the work has just begun.

11 - THE PITCH BOOK

Once you have your partner and are properly incorporated, it's time to find other people's money for your grand experiment. Even with this book as your guide, you want to spend as little of your own money as possible. It is much too risky! Presumably, you still have your full-time job to fund incidental expenses, but now the race is on to nab your first investor. In addition to the business plan, you will need a pitch book.

The pitch book is just another sales tool. You are selling your start-up, and investors are your market. Unlike the business plan, real investors may actually review your pitch book, so it had better look good. To alleviate much of the burden, the intelligent entrepreneur has chosen a partner who is a PowerPoint expert. Since you have already negotiated your ownership percentages, you should let your partner take the lead on pulling together the pitch book. This will build camaraderie and show that you trust them with this important task.

The pitch book is the repackaged business plan. Think of it as a pop-up business plan—full of fun pictures, graphics, and maybe even a video. It contains a summary of each of the five business plan sections in a storytelling format. Indeed, you will need Bill Cosby–like storytelling skills to convince strangers to give you money!

The key to a good pitch book is to produce slides that are not too busy for presentations yet can also be effective without a formal presentation. Like a college freshman out on his own for the first time, the pitch book will end up in awkward places and will have to stand up well alone. The pitch book should be no more than twelve slides long, with a maximum of three slides in the appendix. Bulleted text should be large but sparse on each page. Use the prettiest figures from the business plan. Do not even think about using anything other than a white background for the slides. Above all, keep it simple.

12 - THE ELEVATOR PITCH

Just as a good movie trailer draws in an audience, the elevator pitch should pique the interest of investors and induce questioning. Do not try to do too much here--three sentences are all you should need. If you cannot get a question from someone after a three-sentence description of your amazing company, you either need a communications refresher course or you have followed a bad idea down the rabbit hole. Assuming it is the former, follow some simple rules:

Act like you are not giving an elevator pitch. The goal of the elevator pitch is—like the goal of the business plan—to get the meeting. Be subtle.

"Oh, hello. It's good to run into you, Gus. Say, that reminds me—you may be interested in something I've been working on."

Casually describe the huge problem for which you have found a solution.

"I was amazed to find out that most businesses run into this very same problem thousands of times a day. It's apparently a very big problem."

This will inevitably cause Gus to inquire "So what is so great about your solution?"

You should answer directly while remaining a tease about your secret sauce.

"Well, I've been working with some really sharp people on a solution to this problem, and we think we have it."

Never mention any investment.

"Wow, Gus, it sounds like you might know a lot about this. How about we grab coffee and talk more?"

The astute entrepreneur will notice the progression outlined to this point. It is important! First, you write the business plan, then construct the pitch book, then craft elevator pitch. Never the reverse order! You must build up your venture properly before tearing it down into a refined message.

13 - FIND YOUR ANGELS

You may be tempted to ask your friends and family to invest in your new venture, but this is not recommended. Unless you come from a family with a lot of money, then Mom and Dad are expecting you to ask. But it is best to avoid asking for money from personal relationships. It is the equivalent of being the guy who takes his shirt off in yoga class—you just don't want to be that guy. It is better to source investment from the groups of people out there that enjoy gambling their large disposable incomes on start-ups like yours. They are called angel investors.

Angel investors are like the Sasquatch—shy and rarely seen in public. They are also some of the most accomplished people you will ever come across. The best way to find angel investors is to let them find you. This is where a good start-up attorney earns her keep. Your attorney and your network should be creating a buzz about your new company—all based on buzz that you start with a whisper campaign.

UNCONFIRMED REPORTS OF AN ANGEL INVESTOR AT THE MONSTER START-UP MASHUP
UFO
Angel Investor
Sasquatch
Sightings!
Nightly NEWS

Resist the Urge

They rarely wear name tags, but from time to time you may come across an angel investor at networking events. Tread carefully! Introduce yourself and engage in polite small talk, but resist the urge to discuss your venture in detail. The proper way to engage an angel investor is through an introduction. Use random encounters to set the stage for an introduction later, but never give your elevator pitch to an investor to whom you have not been properly introduced. Such advances show very poor form and will get you nowhere. It is better to be patient and to let them find you after an effective whisper campaign.

Whisper Campaigns

For now, avoid presenting your venture to groups or discussing your venture publicly. Investors like to think they exclusively know stuff that nobody else knows and they derive much joy from their perceived connectivity to the entrepreneurial community. Your new start-up is much more interesting to them when they believe they are the first to know about it. The trick is to make everyone think they are the first to hear about your deal. This is done to maximal effect through a well-thought-out whisper campaign starting with angel investors you know.

"Say, Mr. Dillingham, I wondered if we might have a word in private."

'Sure. What is it, Ollie, my good boy?"

Everyone enjoys the feeling of exclusivity that comes from a "private" conversation.

"Well, I wanted to let you know I've started a new venture."

"You don't say."

Give him your elevator pitch and tell him you would love to get his feedback.

"Please keep this confidential for now."
You really have his interest now! Always ask to keep it confidential. This is a welcome expression of trust and makes the investor feel mighty special.

The window for your whisper campaign is very narrow, so move quickly! The goal of the campaign is to schedule meetings with as many angel investors as possible. The whisper campaign ends as soon as this starts to happen:

"Dillingham, did you know Ollie has started a company? I was talking with him the other day, and it sounds very interesting."

"Of course, met with Ollie last week. Sure is interesting."

Dillingham, of course, is pleased to have known about it first, but the other fellow is quite humiliated. This net zero effect begins to stall out the buzz. At this point, knowledge of your deal has gone mainstream locally, and the whisper campaign is over. Now's the time to deliver your pitch.

14 - THE DOG AND PONY SHOW

The dog and pony show is where you take your pitch book, your partner, and any prototypes on the road to solicit investment. Many first-time entrepreneurs get tripped up here because they think pitching to investors is about communicating a business opportunity. It is not! The pitch is about making investors *feel good.* Learn this lesson and you will go far. The following techniques apply to pitches with angel investors and venture capitalists (VCs) alike.

Deliver Your Pitch

Arrive early, and neatly dressed. Move some piece of furniture in the room. This shows control! Introduce yourself and your partner, but there is no need to let your partner speak. Your partner is there to observe and should sit quietly unless directly addressed. Deliver your well-practiced pitch at a leisurely pace, finishing before your allotted time is up. Remember, the investors are here to feel good, which only happens during the question and answer session (Q&A). Your pitch should perfectly set up the audience for questions.

Some Things Not to Say at a Pitch

"Sorry, I'm a little nervous. This is my first pitch."

"I am currently a tenured professor . . ."

"Robert Kiyosaki always says . . ."

"My wife and I are co-CEOs."

"We all know these projections are meaningless."

Q&A

The most important part of the dog and pony show is the question and answer session. Inexperienced investors are a very insecure bunch, and in groups they ask questions to show their peers how smart they are. Feeling smart is feeling good. You are just a prop for their veiled game of one-upmanship. This is also true of board meetings. But fear not! The enterprising entrepreneur uses this to his advantage.

The trick is to leave the room with everyone feeling that they have asked smart questions or that they have added value. Although this is rarely the case, it can happen. So do pay attention! But do not be discouraged if they try to show off how smart they are at your expense. On the contrary, this is quite desirable. Lie back and attentively take it all in. As long as you do not come across as incompetent, you are in a fine spot.

Do not prepare any backup slides for Q&A; this defeats the point of the pitch meeting entirely. You may think it will show your audience how well prepared you are, but instead it has the effect of making them think they have just asked a common question. Do not let this happen to you! You must make them feel like it is the first time you have ever heard their very insightful question. And if you can't answer a question, this can actually work in your favor. The investor feels like a genius for stumping the teacher and will sleep well tonight.

The smart entrepreneur deliberately leaves key information out of their pitch so that investors can feel good about asking a "critical" question that you "haven't thought of." The content of your answers matters much less than how you frame your response.

"Another really good question!"

"You guys are really keeping me on my toes!"

"Wow, I've never gotten that question before—very good. Let me think about that for a second."

Never let them know that you answer that question a dozen times a week.

The Jerk

"The Jerk" is the name of a great movie and also the investor that really tries to sink his teeth into you. The Jerk will be at any meeting with two or more investors. Be on the lookout for this insecure rascal, for he or she is both aggressive and brutish. The Jerk is quite successful but is terribly insecure and needs constant validation. He or she gets that by putting others down, but do not take it personally.

The Jerk is easy to spot because he or she will ask multiple questions in one breath and will cut you off during your responses. The correct play here is to be steady and super nice. Do not lose your cool! Never challenge the Jerk, instead use him or her to win the sympathies of the other investors who will be thinking, "Here he goes again . . ." The Jerk will try to lure you into an argument, but do not succumb. The Jerk always wins arguments and if he or she does not, the Jerk will lay into you after you have left the room. Instead, the best strategy is to acknowledge the Jerk's current dominant position and deal with him or her later one on one.

"Those are three great questions. We have started to explore how to address those issues but haven't fleshed it out quite yet."

Never give the Jerk your real answers. The Jerk is not interested, and they will never be good enough.

"Good insights! It sounds like you have a lot of experience with this. I look forward to talking with you one on one."

This type of response will greatly please the Jerk.

"I'm sorry, I am not familiar with that, but it sounds like you have some good ideas about this. Perhaps we could chat afterward?"

The Jerk is actually a kitty cat one on one. A private conversation is the best way to win over the Jerk, and once you have, the Jerk will be a staunch behind-the-scenes advocate.

"Yes, I talked to Ollie after the meeting—really a sharp fellow. Of course I set him straight on a few things, but I think he's really on to something here."

THREE PART QUESTION...

Manufacturing Urgency

The best way to combat a weak negotiating position is to create options—even fictitious ones! Getting funded is more like poker than chess. There is a fair amount of bluffing going on. You will hear that raising capital takes a really long time. It does not have to. The trick is to create a sense of urgency with every pitch. Most entrepreneurs miss this important aspect of fundraising. The investor's perspective is "Why invest in a deal today when I can invest in it tomorrow?" Successful entrepreneurs kill that attitude by manufacturing a sense of urgency through the illusion of competition, which preys on the schizophrenic nature of the investor. They do not want to be first, but they are terrified of being left out of a good deal that everyone else is in on.

"Yes, we've had several meetings with Tall and Handsome Capital, and they are quite interested in what we are doing."

Always use "we" even if it was just you—it sounds bigger. No need to mention these meetings were over beers with Gus.

"We are pretty far down the road with Hells Angel Investor Group. We discussed a term sheet just yesterday."

It is OK to say this even if you were the one who initiated the discussion of a term sheet.

"I hope you can move quickly, because it looks like we'll be oversubscribed and will close this by the end of the month."

"Oversubscribed" and "by the end of month" will really get their attention.

"I'm not sure if we are going to take on any new investors. Let me talk with my team and get back to you."

This is a classic disorientation tactic that greatly confuses and excites investors.

15 - SEALING THE DEAL

Be prepared for an avalanche of post-pitch meetings before the seed investment is made. This is normal, as the investor wants to get comfortable with you and would like you to stroke his ego a few more times before paying for it. As talks advance, you will need to show them more of your goodies to maintain interest. It is now appropriate to insist on executing an NDA so you can.

If you have done things properly, you will have several suitors. Continue to subtly play investors off each other, but ultimately you want to pick the investor who can help you get customers the quickest. Look for an investor who is still very active in the sector you are addressing. He or she will have a Rolodex as long as your arm and will be your key to acquiring first customers and future investment.

The novice entrepreneur is distracted by other investor attributes like deep pockets and product development experience. But not you! Take on your angel investor with an eye toward raising the next round of capital at a good valuation, and growing a customer base is key. You also want to pick an angel who is mature enough to handle the

VCs who will be coming in the next round. The last thing you need is an activist angel causing trouble for you later.

Coming to terms with angel investors will be a positive experience because you will not be arguing about the most important term—valuation. Following Congress's methods, why argue today when you can punt and argue later? Instead, you will take your first investment as a convertible note. The note will convert into shares at the valuation the VCs set during the next financing round, with some discount applied to compensate the angel for the risks associated with being early.

You have now come to the end of the beginning of your great story. Well done, but there is much work to do! With money in the bank, it is time to gracefully quit your job and focus on building your disruptive business.

16 - FIRST HIRES MAKE GREAT PETS

You will have raised enough money to support a handful of people for eight to twelve months. This is enough time and manpower to gobble up some important milestones and significantly raise the value of your budding venture. The first operational decisions are upon you: Who should you hire to execute your grand vision?

First hires should be like great pets—obedient, eager to please, and out of your way when you are busy. First hires should not be wantrepreneurs or repeat entrepreneurs. If you hire a wantrepreneur, they will always be distracted by dreams of their own enterprise and may even be bold enough to use your company's resources to set themselves up. Repeat entrepreneurs will ask for too much equity and will be difficult to manage. They know too much! Instead, focus on finding rock-solid technical folks who will get stuff done. These hard workers will be the lifeblood of the company, so choose carefully.

Newly laid-off engineers are particularly desirable as first hires. They are very grateful to have a salary again and they will work for a fair wage. They are a loyal bunch and will be mostly unaffected by the risk of company failure (which is real at this tender stage). While your first hires work tirelessly on product development, preferably reporting to your partner, focus your energies on getting customers.

17 - WHY YOU NEED CUSTOMERS

Despite what you may read in the popular business press, customers are still important to the start-up. Recently it has become in vogue to acquire "users," "hits," "eyeballs," or downloads instead of customers. Ignore this noise, as it leads to fleeting success. It is best to go old school here and focus on real customers for your business. Why? Customers are important because they lead to revenue. Revenues are necessary for profits. Profits are necessary for bigger profits. Big profits are necessary for big success.

Customers, like investors, hate being first or left behind. And your best chance at landing either an investment or a customer is a personal introduction. This is where you leverage the networks of your investors. For this brief moment, you and angels have perfectly aligned goals: making massive amounts of cash. Leverage this brief moment of total alignment and get them to help you sell your product.

Getting your first customer to pay for anything is damn near impossible. You are a start-up, unproven and raw. Your first customers are smart enough to know they are guinea pigs and there is value in them showing up, so you will have to give away lots of product and services for free before they pay you a dime. But do not be discouraged. This is why you have investors—to carry you through the lean times. This is also when having a "sticky" product pays off. You get them hooked for free, then their cost to cancel or change becomes too great.

With these early customers, you must get them to agree that you can publicly use their name. This has tremendous value in creating buzz. Focus on creating the perception that your product offering is special, and other customers will start to wonder what they are missing.

At this point, do not worry about earning much revenue from customers. For now, customers are like kitty litter in the snow—they help you get traction. At this early stage, customers are merely pitch book candy for the Series A dog and pony show, so get the biggest names and go for high volume. Nabbing paying customers comes later; Series A money is used for acquiring them.

18 - SEDUCING THE VC

A month after closing your angel round, you need to start raising more money to feed your quickly growing venture. Fund-raising will be a big part of your life for the next several years, so pucker up, kid! Big visions like yours require large amounts of capital, and only VCs can supply that kind of money.

You may think that venture capitalists are like gods, sitting on piles of cash and answering to no one. This is a common misperception. Peel back the layers, and you will find that VCs actually answer to Limited Partners (LPs). Like the yellow sun is to Superman, the limited partner is the source of the VC's superpowers. They provide the capital for VCs to invest, dress nicely, and have fancy cars. LPs are typically high net worth individuals, pension funds, or university endowments. Without the LP, the VC is just like every other man, only whiter. Unfortunately, the VC industry is less diverse than the National Hockey League.

Another feature to understand about your VC target is the following: VCs never voluntarily leave the business. They either die or are forced out because they cannot raise another fund. Understand this, and you will go far with this intelligent bunch! A VC's every move is choreographed to raise his next fund so he can keep being a VC. That is all they ever want for Christmas—to keep on being a VC. Because it is probably the greatest job on the planet, and it pays really well if you are good at it (and even if you're not).

There are only two ways for a VC to raise the next fund: 1) by having great real returns to investors or 2) by making convincing arguments about the estimated gains of portfolio companies from their first fund (google J-Curve). The latter allows clever VCs to always raise at least two funds, regardless of their ability to make investors money.

Like angel investors, VCs are pack animals. Fear drives their pack mentality. They call their packs "syndicates." If you are going to look stupid, it is better to look stupid while standing in a group with your good-looking friends who also look stupid at the time. This also explains why there are so few leaders in the VC community. Everyone's looking for cover in case an investment fails. But in you they will see their next billion-dollar success—and aren't they special for finding you? When VC's stumble upon good deals, they call it "proprietary deal flow." Feed their talent-finding egos and you will win their hearts.

But it is darn tough to get a VC excited. They have heard it all. They are constantly being lied to by young whippersnappers with low moral fiber. And they hate to invest in first-time entrepreneurs. The only way to overcome this bias is by gaining massive traction fast—either through impressive revenues or numbers of customers. If you have either, you will be the belle of the ball with your choice of worthy suitors. If you have neither—and these are difficult to fake—you must fabricate some new, albeit vague, form of traction. The answer to every investor question during the Series A capital raise is always "traction."

Remember that you do not just want a VC for the money. Partnering with a VC just for the money is like getting married for the sex. There are plenty of other ways to get either with much less aggravation. Instead, the worthy VC should be your ticket to big-time customers and even bigger investors for later rounds. Always be thinking of raising your next round of capital!

The Value of Venture Conferences

If you really want to get term sheets fast, present at a venture conference but only under the guise that you "are not looking for any additional investors at this time." Venture conferences are only good for one thing: creating competition for your deal. Only agree to present at a venture conference after you have at least one term sheet.

You will deliver a brilliant marketing pitch that is short on details but long on projections and marketing fluff. The audience will have a ton of questions, but you will not directly answer any of them. Always end your pitch by mentioning the top-notch firms with which you are talking, without using specific names. It is also proper to say something like: "I'll be happy to speak with you more if you have questions, but we're not looking for any new investors."

This is a good example of turning the tables on VCs during your courtship. They love a good chase, and you can gain their attention by not returning phone calls, ignoring their e-mails, and generally acting disinterested in them. Make it known that you have several suitors and that competitive term sheets are imminent. For the uninitiated, a term sheet is a cheat sheet for VCs. It summarizes the terms under which they intend to make an investment.

"Ollie, we've been trying to get in touch with you about participating in the Series A."

"Yes, I'm terribly sorry, Gus. We've been so busy lately."

"I heard you've been talking with the guys at Engorged Venture Partners."

"Indeed—a sharp group of guys over there. We're expecting a term sheet any day, Gus."

"Well, just wait before you sign anything, Ollie. Tall and Handsome Capital is the right firm for you, and we'll have you a term sheet by the end of the week."

WE ARE NOT LOOKING FOR INVESTMENT AT THIS TIME
Dead Cat Inc.

19 - NEGOTIATING A TERM SHEET

It is an odd thing, negotiating a term sheet, namely because your adversary is the VC that you just fell in love with. It is like negotiating a prenuptial agreement right after you propose—very awkward. But this is one of your most important jobs as CEO, and the terms you agree to will affect company structure, control, future investment, and payouts. Before engaging in negotiations, you should educate yourself using the many good term sheet resources available to the entrepreneur. The Google machine will provide many good suggestions. Here we discuss a few key considerations, with the main points being: 1) don't get too hung up on the valuation and 2) check your lawyer's work.

How to Calculate a Pre-Money Valuation

Regarding company valuation, here is a good phrase to keep in your pocket: "Our existing investors and management team have a number in mind based on the technology, team, market size, and progress to date." Always reference your responsibility to others. An even better answer is: "We have a term sheet that values us at $x million, so there's the floor." When you have a term sheet in hand, you have an opportunity to flex what is known as your "Term Sheet Muscles."

If you are still developing Term Sheet Muscles, then just back into a reasonable pre-money valuation. Figure out the return that would be very good—but reasonable—for your VC investors based on the ownership percentage they will have after the last round of financing. Do a little research on comparable companies to see what multiple of EBITDA is typical for acquisitions in your space. Solve for your first investors receiving seven times their money after seven years, and you can figure out at what valuation they have to invest in to receive this return. This is your pre-money valuation. If you do not follow the math here, then have your cofounder do it. If you cannot make the numbers work for at least a sevenfold return for your initial investors, go back to Chapter 2, because you have picked the wrong idea!

Valuation is an important aspect of term sheets, but it gets too much attention as the deal headliner. There are several other levers in the term sheet that can be adjusted to account for a high or low valuation. A long-standing investor maxim is "My valuation under your terms or your valuation under my terms – you can't have both."

Stack the BOD

Five is a nice number for a board of directors at this stage—two from your side, one from each investor, and one independent that you appoint. Six would work, too. Do not worry about having an even number. If a board decision requires a tiebreaker, your company has much bigger issues.

Don't forget: You report to the board. When agreeing to a BOD, always remember that some day, after rounds of dilution, the board will most likely have the ability to fire you. Avoid this situation by having competitive term sheets so you can hold on to controlling shares, even if you are not the majority shareholder. If this is not possible, then stack the board with investors and independent people that you genuinely trust. This is your chance to pick the group of people who will fire you, and—like every great entrepreneur—you want to be fired by only the best.

Once your BOD is in place, never try to actually decide anything during a board meeting. Decisions are made by you before and after board meetings. Board meetings are for exposing the consensus you have built around your decisions so that all feel involved.

Vesting

Wikipedia.com says that in law, vesting is to give an immediately secured right of present or future enjoyment. In other words, vesting is a pair of investor handcuffs. Vesting schedules are used to deliver shares to you and key members of your team over time—typically four years—to ensure that there is continued incentive for you to keep working hard. If you own 40 percent of the company and your shares vest over four years, you accumulate actual ownership of your shares at a rate of 10 percent per year. Some VCs have the balls to ask you to reset your vesting schedule based on the date of their investment. Politely ask them if they might like a nice, hot cup of go-screw-yourself. Resetting the vesting schedule is not something you can do to your team (always cite your responsibility to the team). You have a vesting schedule in place from the angel round of financing, and it is disingenuous of them to ask you to start over again.

Other Terms

Vanishing liquidation preferences, right of first refusal, anti-dilution, no-shop provisions, redemption rights—these are not just terms used to impress at MBA disco night. You must read and understand everything in the term sheet before signing. Do not rely on your lawyer to protect you. Odds are that you are smarter than your lawyer. You are the one with everything on the line, so you are ultimately responsible for knowing what you are signing.

20 - THE POWER OF PRESS RELEASES

Press releases are a wonderful tool for disseminating carefully crafted fictions about you and your company. Early on, they are great masterpieces of your creative writing skills. Later, you will need to outsource this fun activity to professionals so you can focus on other things.

A well-written press release can make something as trivial as the relocation of an office sound impressive. Be sure to mention your company name early and often. One exercise that is useful in gauging the effectiveness of your press release is to replace your company name with the name of a BigCo. If you finish reading the press release and it sounds like something a BigCo would put out, you have a winner! Below is an example of a product press release:

>>>>>

Los Angeles, Calif., April 6, 2013 /PRNewswire/ -- Dead Cat, Inc., today announced a new, complete alternative software suite called Bounce™ to power its customer relationship management software. Bounce™ is a highly intelligent yet simple and effective tool based on proprietary algorithms. Dead Cat's Bounce™ represents the next generation of sustainable CRM systems currently used by many Fortune 500 companies. The announcement was made during a product launch reception at the All Things Digital Conference in Rancho Palos Verdes, California.

Dead Cat's Bounce™ offers numerous benefits as an alternative to traditional CRM software. Bounce™ mirrors the exceptional performance qualities of imbedded CRM programs while also delivering a number of excellent database management benefits—including a 51 percent increase in efficiency and the ability to increase repeat sales by over 74 percent. Dead Cat plans to commercialize Bounce-Light™ for small businesses in 2015.

"We are proud to be a leader in providing alternative and disruptive CRM solutions to the market," said Oliver Chesterfield, President and CEO of Dead Cat, Inc. "It is clear that Dead Cat's Bounce™ technology offers great value for corporate clients and is the latest example of our commitment to our customers." The announcement highlights Dead Cat, Inc.'s ongoing dedication to developing alternative CRM drivelines to responsibly synchronize sales, marketing, and customer service functions.

>>>>>

Because it appears on the web and looks professional, people take notice. Even if nobody has a clue what the announcement is about, it will be picked up by news groups across the country. And it will get your brand out there, which is the whole point. Be like Donald Trump with your press releases: shameless in your self-promotion.

21 - BREAKING UP WITH YOUR COFOUNDER

Here's an unwritten start-up rule: If it isn't going well, blame your cofounder. Understand that if you can't blame your cofounder, the board will blame you. And then your job is in jeopardy, which threatens the whole venture. So a good CEO will do what is right for investors, employees, and customers and fire their cofounder when the going gets tough. Although the pain will be palpable for a long time, your cofounder will forgive you many years later once you have made them wealthy. And if that doesn't happen, well, they never should have left!

You know it is time to part ways with your partner when you have clearly grown apart and argue more than you laugh. You live and breathe the business, but your partner—not so much. Your cofounder has become more of a nuisance than a help. He is constantly looking for ways to insert himself into critical company operations where his contribution is negligible. Or maybe she shows up to meetings she is not invited to. Regardless, their negative attitude is bringing everyone down. You need to get away from each other. It is time to do what's best for the company.

“You wanted to see me, Ollie?”

“Yes, Pincus, please close the door and sit down.”

“OK. What’s up?”

“We both know it has been a rough time lately, and you have been very unhappy. Perhaps it’s time for us to look into having you do something different for a while.”

“What? Where is this coming from?”

He shifts to the front edge of his chair, and his up-inflection rips through your eardrum. But you are steady.

“Yes, it is clear to everyone that you’re very unhappy and something needs to change. Is there anything you want to talk about?”

“No, not really. I know we have not been getting along, but that happens. There is nothing wrong.”

“Well, the board feels it might be best if you take a break from Dead Cat, Inc., for a while to regroup.”

“The Board!?”

His eyes are bigger than a pair of half-eaten Cadbury eggs.

“Pincus, it’s nobody’s fault. It’s not you. The business has changed.”

“Are you crazy? I’ve just been focusing on the things you’ve told me to focus on!”

You are saddened by his shameful ignorance.

"I know, and believe me, that's what makes this even harder."

Spend some time grieving with your partner and absorbing the obscenities that will follow. Then send him or her home for the weekend and get to work on the press release, which should be used to your advantage. Focus on the accomplishments of your partner's replacement while praising your ex-partner for helping to guide the company through a critical growth stage. Express regret that the company is losing him or her "for family reasons." Send out the press release and then move on. It is time to focus on raising more capital.

YOU'RE FIRED
IT'S NOT YOU, IT'S ME

22 - THE SERIES B CLUB

Congratulations! You have survived the grueling demands of a growing start-up. You have successfully managed to get buy-in from early customers, investors, and employees. You have successfully introduced products that are selling like hotcakes. You have revenues. Your headcount approaches thirty. You are a darling of the technology world. You have been asked to do a TED Talk. You have networked your way into the hearts of angel investors and VCs alike. You have done well by any measure, but there's no time to slow down. Now it's time to raise Series B capital to scale your shit fast.

Try to enjoy yourself during the Series B road show. Your Series A investors will do much of the heavy lifting; they now have great incentive to get more money into the deal at a higher valuation. They will work their networks and make you look better than Kate Moss next to Johnny Depp. This is where all of your press releases and manufactured buzz around your deal pay big dividends. And because it is so easy to double revenues in the early days, your revenue growth will look juicy. New investors are clamoring to hear your story and look at the numbers—and they are impressive!

"You guys should take a look at Dead Cat, Inc.—one of our portfolio companies that is just crushing it."

"Thanks for telling me about it, Gus. What do they do?"

"They kill it every day."

"What's the round look like?"

"Looks like it is going to be oversubscribed, but we would be willing to carve out a piece if you all can move fast."

"Gus, I really appreciate that. Pompis Ventures is definitely interested."

At this point, you may take some time to reflect and compare yourself to some of your counterparts who have attempted this journey without this guide. You notice they have alienated their closest friends. Their spouses resent their start-ups. Their bodies have atrophied to resemble that of a meth addict. For them, the closing of the Series B capital raise promises the opportunity to work harder, take on even more responsibility, and further damage more personal relationships. But not you! With this guide safely tucked into your pocket, the fun continues. Enjoy the flood of well-wishes that will come after the press release goes out.

>>>>>

San Jose, CA, October 10, 2013 /PRNewswire/ — Dead Cat, Inc., announced today that the company has raised $10 million in Series B funding from current investors Tall and Handsome Capital, Engorged Venture Partners, and Pompis

Ventures. The investment will accelerate the introduction of Bounce™, Dead Cat's first product, into the market. Dead Cat's Bounce™ is a CRM-enhanced productivity tool that is an ultra-low cost, drop-in replacement for large enterprise solutions.

"When we invest, we are looking for the best companies with the best teams that have disruptive technologies for very large markets," said Augustine S. "Gus" Huckabee, General Partner at Tall and Handsome Capital. "The next generation CRM market is a multi-billion dollar market that continues to grow. The cost advantage of Bounce™ and its cutting-edge virtual approach puts Dead Cat in a leadership position to deliver solutions to increasingly higher value segments of the supply chain."

"We appreciate the continued confidence from our Tier 1 group of investors," said Oliver Chesterfield, President and CEO of Dead Cat, Inc. "We have made significant progress in the development of our disruptive Phase II CRM technology, and our customers will see dramatic benefits from Bounce™ that will enable them to grow their revenue and improve margins."

>>>>>

23 - SERIES C SHOPPING SPREE

If the Series B capital is the fuel for your exponential growth, the Series C is the nitrous oxide kicker that really launches your company to the next level. When thinking about the Series C capital raise, approach it like a shopping spree. Think of all of the fun things you would do if you only had the money. Series C capital is for those things! It allows you to fly business class to Europe or China so you can start developing international markets. You can finally beef up your sales team and get that personal assistant you so desperately need. And do not forget facility upgrades; now you can move into a much nicer, roomier facility downtown to accommodate your growing team. Oh, and a proper marketing budget! Imagine how fast you will grow with a proper marketing budget! Treat yourself.

Securing Series C investment is your reward for proving your business model and crossing the Valley of Death. Now you must bulk up your balance sheet to grow even faster. This is important because your success and buzz has attracted Dead Cat copycats funded by deep-pocketed me-too VCs. You can coolly address the increased competition through acqui-hires. Use the Series C windfall to acquire one or two smaller—but very capable—copycat companies that have been stealing headlines and customers from you. The result will be that you tighten your grip over this new market. Bulk up while you can, because you will need your strength to combat the BigCos that have finally realized you are a threat to their business.

The Series C investment involves much bigger money, and so you will need to attract investors with deeper pockets and a lower risk tolerance. These downstream VCs are cut from the same mold as your earlier investors, so they are easy enough to manage. And because your deal has been significantly de-risked, your valuation will be high enough to stomach the extra dilution. But make no mistake: You need their cash! You are entering a sprint to the finish line and will need all of the resources you can muster to get to the exit.

24 - THE EXIT

Your revenues are growing exponentially. You are profitable. You are hitting your numbers. You do not need any more capital. Investment bankers keep calling you. When these things align, the smart entrepreneur starts looking for the door.

How to Get Acquired

It is time to make amends with the old-guard BigCos that you abhor and have been stealing business from for years. They are late to the party. They know it. You know it. There is now a billion-dollar market that you have created from scratch. It could have been theirs if only they were nimble enough. But they are not. And they never will be. They are drowning in bureaucracy, and they are a mess. But they have cash-cow products, robust distribution, and a good brand name to inefficiently make big money. The good news is that they don't know how to innovate, so they buy you.

Acquiring Dead Cat, Inc., is the only way BigCo can grow, expand its margins, and keep its shareholders happy. BigCo will overpay for your company to prevent one of its competitors from acquiring you. It wants the essence of your organization to infuse new life into its aging business. Dead Cat, Inc., is the new marrow in a bone marrow transplant, and—to BigCo—it is worth the expense.

Start the process by having your investment banking suitors make overtures to the M&A groups of several BigCos. Start by agreeing to some preliminary calls, and let the bankers handle the courting process. Flirt a little and show some interest before entertaining serious talks.

Threaten to IPO

The smart entrepreneur does not really want to be the CEO of a public company. It is way better to be acquired and forced out after an awkward six months at BigCo. The rigors of running a public company are not typically aligned with the skill set, passions, and free-wheeling style of the entrepreneur who built the company from scratch. Very few have made this transition successfully. You must come to terms with the fact that exceptional human beings like Bill Gates and Mark Zuckerberg are outliers of outliers. Instead, use the threat of a public offering to drive up your acquisition price. It will also give you a chance to spend some good, quality time with investment bankers at excellent strip clubs.

25 - SCREW-YOU MONEY

The excitement of the acquisition will eventually die down, and you will find yourself introspective. Reflecting on the wild, beautiful ride you have just taken, you exhale. That was fun. One thousand things went right. Ten thousand things went wrong. But you did it. Everyone wants to know what you are going to do next. The answer is, "Whatever the hell I want."

To really give an answer like that—and mean it—you must have made a substantial amount of money from the exit event. How much? You'll know it when you see it. It is called "screw-you money." If you have that kind of money, you don't have to call people back, because you don't give a damn if they keep calling or not. It is the end of putting up with bullshit as you know it. You have graduated to a distributor from a receiver in the Circle of Bullshit.

The Circle of Bullshit has existed since the dawn of humankind and is fueled by screw-you money. You start off as an eager beaver trying to get things done and wondering why people don't return your messages sooner. You swear that once you make it you will never treat people this way. Then you struggle through the next decade of your career getting pissed off because guys higher than you are unresponsive. You curse their names and swear to extract revenge. Years later you achieve great success and true financial security. You stop returning calls because you can, even though the people you are hurting have had no hand in your past bad experiences. The people you now snub swear that once they make it they will never treat people this way. And the Circle of Bullshit continues.

The Circle of Bullshit!
Newcomers
I am trying to make things happen. Why is this guy not returning my calls?
Nobody is returning my calls. I will never be like this.
It is rude to be so unresponsive; I am officially pissed. Someday I will have my revenge.
I have screw you money. I do not feel like responding to people anymore.
Screw You Money!

26 - BANG! YOU ARE A BRAND AND A MENTOR

You have earned massive street credibility among wantrepreneurs, entrepreneurs, investors, and corporate climbers. By accident rather than by design, you have created a distinct personal brand, which is "I am that guy who had a very successful exit and I do not need to work anymore." People will be clamoring to know how you did it. No need to mention this book—much better for others to discover it for themselves. Instead, talk about how blessed you have been. It will only add to the intrigue.

An unfortunate product of your success is that people will want your opinion on climate change, world peace, feeding the poor, and all of the other big-issue problems of the day. You will be a sought-after board member. Universities will want you on their faculty. Celebrities will want to dine with you. Publishers will want to bottle your success. Politicians will want your endorsement and your money. It is best to steer clear of these distractions, as they serve only to diminish your brand.

"Ollie, what would it take to make you a partner here at Tall and Handsome Capital?"

"Gee, Gus, I'm flattered. But I'm going to take a little break for while."

"OK. Just let us know when you're ready."

Of course, you will never be ready. If you do want to go play VC, you will surely do it as a founding partner of your own shop. But no need to say this. It is better to just play the fade.

"Impressive run, Ollie, very impressive."

"Thank you, Mr. Stackhouse."

"We sure could use a guy like you on the Board of Stackhouse Industries."

"That's very nice of you to say, sir, but I'm taking some time off to be with my family."

"Good boy, Ollie. We'll be here when you're ready."

While board duty for a BigCo would stroke your ego and is light duty, you do not need the aggravation. You'll have much more fun leveraging your brand as a mentor, adviser, and investor. In any case, you will get dozens of similar offers.

As a mentor and adviser, your gift to the world is as a thought leader on entrepreneurship. You start a blog to educate the masses about how you succeeded. It accidently becomes a way to promote yourself and your books and graciously teach entrepreneurs start-up etiquette. As an investor, your gift is to make even more money for future philanthropic endeavors. And it is much easier now to make money, because the game is rigged in your favor. You will see the best deals and have access to the sweetest terms, because your name on a capitalization table is more valuable than your investment dollars. This in turn attracts the best opportunities and the best people to your investments, greatly increasing success rates. But be wary of the enterprising first-time entrepreneur who asks you in an elevator, "Ollie, might I have a word in private? I wanted to tell you about a new venture I've been working on. . . ."

27 - GLOSSARY FOR ENTREPRENEURS

Angel Investor – An accomplished and wealthy individual with a lot more money than you. They enjoy investing in start-up companies and can easily absorb a total loss of their investment, which is likely.

EBITDA – Earnings Before Interest, Taxes, Depreciation and Amortization. A boring accounting term that gives a more accurate picture of a company's profitability. People like it because you can compare performance across industries and it neutralizes financing shenanigans.

Elevator Pitch – The story you tell about your business that gets you a meeting. It is the entrepreneur's two minute summary of the business opportunity. It had better be good.

Limited Partner (LP) – The top of the food chain, they are the true drivers of the venture capital industry. They are high net worth individuals, pension funds, insurance companies, foundations, university endowments, and funds of funds. LPs provide the capital for VCs to invest in early stage companies. They are rarely seen in public.

Non-Disclosure Agreement (NDA) – Also known as a Confidentiality Agreement (CA), this legal document binds the signers to maintain the secrecy of shared confidential information. The NDA is typically executed with investors only after a lengthy courting process. Even with an NDA in place, be careful what you share with tire-kickers.

Pain Point – This is the problem—known or unknown—that your business solves for customers. New solutions to widespread pain points can create huge value.

Pitch Book – A sales document that summarizes your business opportunity and markets it to investors. Full of assumptions and optimism, it presents a version of the future that excites investors and compels them to learn more. It is a tool to get more meetings.

PPM: Private Placement Memorandum – Things are getting serious once a PPM is drafted. It is the equivalent of a prospectus for public companies and covers your ass with the SEC. It's basically a longer and fancier version of your business plan. The PPM describes objectives, risks and terms of the investment at length.

Proprietary Deal Flow – A term made up by VC's to justify their high fees. "Generating proprietary deal flow" is also referred to as a VC doing his job.

Screw-you Money – Add to the chip on your shoulder a large amount of money accumulated through hard work, luck, and business savvy, and you end up with screw-you money. Having that kind of money means that you will never have to return calls or say you're sorry again.

Secret Sauce – This is the thing that you do or make that is the key to your success and cannot be easily replicated. It's what makes your company special and destined for greatness.

Syndicate – The formal name for a pack of investors that pool their money and invest in your start-up company. Syndicates are very fragile and can appear and vaporize suddenly.

Term Sheet – A summary of the investment terms under which an investor will make an investment. Coming to an agreement on a Term Sheet is a difficult but major milestone.

Term Sheet Muscles – This is what you grow once you have a Term Sheet with an investor. Flexing your Term Sheet Muscles will attract other investors.

Valuation – This is how much your company is worth. Determining the company valuation is more art than science. Assigning an exact monetary value is a negotiation and is only relevant during fundraising and exit. At all other times, just be sure it is increasing.

Valley of Death – Every company goes through it, but many don't survive the trip. It is the period between securing investments and having enough recurring revenue to sustain yourself.

Venture Capitalist – They get paid to invest other people's money in high risk/high reward young companies. Great VCs are really good at judging talent and predicting the future. Bad ones are great salesmen.

Vesting – A tool to make sure the early management team is not dead weight. Vesting requires you to earn into your equity over four years or so, to ensure you don't leave early with a bag full of equity.

Wantrepreneur – Your sister, your brother, your mother and your father. They are everywhere. Wantrepreneurs talk like they are entrepreneurs, but they haven't done a single entrepreneurial thing…yet.

Whisper Campaign – This is the flurry of activity that creates buzz around your start-up. A good whisper campaign can fabricate interest from thin air. Timing is everything.

ACKNOWLEDGMENTS

Inspiration comes from strange places and people, and I'd like to especially thank all of those strange people. Too numerous to list, you are the grinders that make entrepreneurship look easy. You keep going because it's part of who you are. We usually don't hear about you until many years later, although you've been successful for a long time because you do your own thing. You have a unique view of the world that drives you and sparks the imaginations of others. You are the true entrepreneurs. You create, build, fail again and again, and get things done. Most importantly, you inspire the next generation of entrepreneurs.

Special thanks to Susan, Andy, and Tony for helping to make this book better through their valuable feedback.

www.ingramcontent.com/pod-product-compliance
Lightning Source LLC
Chambersburg PA
CBHW051335170526
45166CB00002B/827
* 9 7 8 1 4 9 3 5 0 5 5 0 0 *